Well Done

Well Done

The Journey of a Well-Doer

TIKITA C. PEAGLER

XULON PRESS

Xulon Press
2301 Lucien Way #415
Maitland, FL 32751
407.339.4217
www.xulonpress.com

Unless otherwise indicated, Scripture quotations taken from the King James Version (KJV)–public domain.

Scripture quotations taken from the New King James Version (NKJV). Copyright © 1982 by Thomas Nelson, Inc. Used by permission. All rights reserved.

Scripture quotations taken from The Message (MSG). Copyright © 1993, 1994, 1995, 1996, 2000, 2001, 2002. Used by permission of NavPress Publishing Group. Used by permission. All rights reserved.

Scripture quotations taken from the Holy Bible, New International Version (NIV). Copyright © 1973, 1978, 1984, 2011 by Biblica, Inc.™. Used by permission. All rights reserved.

Scripture quotations taken from the Common English Bible® (CEB) Copyright © 2010, 2011 by Common English Bible.™ Used by permission. All rights reserved worldwide.

Scripture quotations taken from the Holy Bible, New Living Translation (NLT). Copyright ©1996, 2004, 2007 by Tyndale House Foundation. Used by permission of Tyndale House Publishers, Inc.

Printed in the United States of America.

Paperback ISBN-13: 978-1-63221-764-6
eBook ISBN-13: 978-1-6322-1765-3

DEDICATION

To my mother, late grandmother Loretta, Aunt Viola, and nine *Davis* aunts, thank you for loving me deeply and investing into who I would become. You have inspired me to journey this life well.

To the loves of my life: Madison, Joshua, and Caleb, I love you beyond words and I am so proud of you!

And Jeremy, what can I say? You continue to take my breath away. I love you.

FOREWORD

I am not sure about you, but from as early as I can remember, I always had a desire to do everything in my life as perfectly as I could. Striving for perfection had become the measuring stick of achievement in my mind. In my pursuit of perfection, I looked for affirmation that I was doing the right thing through the lenses of my parents, teachers, and anyone through my life's journey that I esteemed highly. Hearing the phrases, "good job," "I am proud of you," and "well-done" became the badges of honor I continued to seek without fail. However, when I'd fail short of what I thought was the expectation, a self-defeating demeanor overtook the very core of my being.

I must say even now, in my mid-forties, there are still some struggles of trying to be perfect in every area of my life: whether it is as a woman, maintaining the perfect weight; as a mother, assuring that my children are perfect without flaws and following the path that I have created in my mind; as a wife, assuring that my husband and I continue to not only love each other but like each other, and the list goes on and on. It had come to a point where I realized that my pursuit for perfection was misguided. Wanting to do well had become a race in being a people-pleaser and not acknowledging that God was, and is, the person in which I should be looking to as a well-doer. Now do not get me wrong; we need people in our lives to assist us in navigating through our day-to-day experiences, but we should not put them in a place that is only reserved for God.

As I sat intently engaging in Tikita's new book, "Well-Done," I found myself reflecting on the very aspects of my life that I have given over to God while, on the other hand, recognizing that there are still some areas I tend to hold on to. You and I must never forget the faithfulness of our Father: being gracious to ourselves just as God has extended grace to us; remaining tender-hearted and not allowing the cares of this world to taint the pureness within us; and ultimately making sure that our lives are in continual pursuit of God's purpose for our lives.

Within the pages of this book, you will be given an opportunity to interact by taking a moment to pause and reflect on God's goodness. In addition, you will have multiple times to address those areas of your life that can be hinderances to being a well-doer. I am a witness of Tikita's life, as she whole-heartedly pursues to live a life that is pleasing to God. In her continual pursuit in touching the lives of women around the world, this book, "Well-Done," is penned from a place where you will be given godly principles, a prayer of encouragement at the conclusion of each chapter, and a time of reflection. In the end, Tikita's desire is for everyone to be a "well-doer." So, let the journey begin.

Kierston Bartney

Dynasty Empowerment Center, Pastor

Author of Protectors of the Covenant

I have known Tikita Peagler for over a decade, as co-laborers with Christ and servant leaders in God's kingdom. I have always found her to be an exceptional woman of God with incredible wisdom, unquestionable character, and deep core convictions that are rooted in Christ. So, when I was asked to write a foreword for her second book, I was truly honored. It is not often that one is asked to be a part of such legacy-defining achievements, such as authoring and publishing not one but two literary works that are spiritual gems.

Over the past twelve years, I have had the pleasure of witnessing Tikita mentor, counsel, and nurture women of all ages, races, ethnicities, and socioeconomic statuses. She has been remarkably blessed by God with an incredible gift to connect and gain influence in a way that allows her to help others journey well in their spiritual walk with the Lord. Her tender heart for others, and her love for God and His people, is why I'm certain that Well Done will overwhelmingly resonant with the readers.

As Tikita shared her own private journey through the lessons of life that brought her closer to Jesus, I personally found myself deeply moved and reinvigorated with energy and strength to hear, "Well done! You are a good and faithful servant. You've been faithful over a little. I'll put you in charge of much. Come, celebrate with me" (Matt. 25:23 CEB). I pray that you too will be moved by the treasured principles shared within these pages, the creative accounts of biblical stories, and the renewing power of the Holy Spirit.

Elder Anton Stiles, BS, MA
United Christian Ministers Association
Oklahoma City, OK

TABLE OF CONTENTS

INTRODUCTION:
THE WELL-DOER

According to economist, Max Roser, life expectancy has increased rapidly since the 18th Century (Max Roser, 2013). Research suggests that in a pre-modern, poor world, life expectancy was around thirty years in all regions of the world. In the 1900s, the global average life expectancy more than doubled and steadied close to seventy years. Fast forward, the current life expectancy for world citizens in 2020 is 72.63 years (Macrotrends, 2020). The reality of the matter is, we are born and then we die. And if we are fortunate, we are granted significant time and space between those two main events. That space is often colorful and hugely emotional, a canvas painted only by the intricacies of life.

It is both intriguing and painful to comprehend the fact people like King David, Abraham Lincoln, Maya Angelo, Madam C.J. Walker, Mother Teresa, Michael Jackson, or even my Great-Grandmother Lucetta Riley, lived full lives like you and me, but are no longer here. This is a sober reminder that someday I too will be a memory. These individuals experienced the carefree heart of a child, the self-awareness season of a teenager, the explorative years of their twenties, and felt the weight of responsibility of their thirties. Each of these seasons were filled with minutes of hours, days, and months. They lived their lives. Yet, their journey on planet earth had an expiration date and came to an end. God gave each of them a journey to travel, a life to explore, and a story to create.

I'm reminded of the promise God gave Moses to share with the Children of Israel as they journeyed to the Promised Land from Egypt. Moses reported that God had set before the Israelites life and prosperity, death and destruction, and they were free to choose with the understanding that each path held an obvious consequence. This promise was not only to the Israelites, but it is a law that God has established in the earth and applies to all mankind. With this knowledge, I am particularly interested in the holy women of faith described by the Apostle Peter in 1 Peter 3: 5-6, as women who pleased God because they were not fearful, and they were well-doers. In essence, life's circumstances did not make them afraid because they trusted in God; thus, they lived life well and did good. These women chose the good part of the promise—life and prosperity, and subsequently, reaped the blessing of legacy and trend-setting for generations of women to follow.

In my inaugural book, *Undisturbed*, I talked about Sarah, whom the Apostle Peter described as the example of a woman who adorned her heart with a meek and undisturbed spirit, which is priceless to God. I was so excited to discover that it pleases God if I walk in humility and don't allow life to disturb me, due to an unyielding faith in Him. Sarah inspired me to trust God and endeavor to never be afraid.

I must be honest. Living undisturbed in such a colorful world where circumstances can change at a moment's notice isn't always easy; however, it is possible and so rewarding. Yet, there is so much in between the moments of life ... the minutes, hours, days, months, and years. Undoubtedly, this life will present you and me with both good and bad, sunshine and rain. How do we navigate? The Apostle Peter said that the holy women of old journeyed this life free from the grip of fear and they journeyed well. They were described as well-doers. Women who went about living life well and doing good despite the complexities of life. I don't know about you, but I desire to have the testimony of being a well-doer and having lived this life well. The Holy Scripture ascribes that God will say on judgement day to those who kept the faith, "well done, good and faithful servant."

I would like to invite you on my journey to live my life well. Along the way, I hope you discover treasured principles that inspire you to be a well-doer—a soul who lives life well.

> *"His master replied, 'Well done! You are a good and faithful servant. You've been faithful over a little. I'll put you in charge of much. Come, celebrate with me.'*
> *Matthew 25:23 CEB*

Chapter One

The Well-Doer
LISTENS

Oh, how I needed this cup of coffee this morning. For the last couple of months, I have been laying off coffee and substituting it with green tea instead. But today was a different story.

There are some days when we are just tired... physically and emotionally, and today was that day. As I have matured and traversed the paths of this life, I have discovered that it is okay to be tired. As a woman, this revelation can be hard to accept. Especially if you are wired like me and you are a "get it done-systematic" type gal. Truly, there are methods for accomplishing the steps in my plan and getting tired is not one of them.

While in prayer this past weekend, I immediately began rambling off my prayer request to the Lord. I did not get very far before the Lord gently interrupted me and whispered, *"Faith without hearing is impossible."* I pondered on this statement for a long moment and then replied, *"Amen... I agree Lord."* You see, the Bible says that faith's exposure to mankind happens through hearing ... faith comes by hearing and hearing by the Word of God (Rom. 10:17). Case in point, I was tired, and God knew it. Yet, He had something to share with me that He discerned my soul so desperately needed to hear. No prayer required, just a yielded heart and listening ear, all that my faith may be increased.

A modern-day shepherd in Israel recently said that shepherds do not generally make their sheep lie down by physical force nor by verbal instruction. Sheep will lie down in green pastures typically when they feel safe and feel no threat of predators. You see, when I went into prayer, I was worried about many things and could hardly wait to get before the Lord so that I could systematically ramble off my concerns to Him. However, the above principle admonishes me that if I, like the sheep, trust Him whole-heartedly with no fear of the predator of life, I too, can rest in green pastures and be at peace. Sheep rest because of the presence of a reliable shepherd; they trust his guidance and protection. If there should be any danger, they would hear the shepherd's voice of warning and follow his guidance. I am so glad that I listened when God interrupted my prayer that morning, and His words encouraged my heart. I left prayer knowing that all was well. I now understand it is okay to be tired; the Good Shepherd knows and allows me to rest in green pastures until I get a second wind.

He maketh me to lie down in green pastures: he leadeth me beside the still waters. Psalm 23:2 KJV

Do you remember the time Martha had the privilege of hosting Jesus in her home? Jesus had just finished teaching, appointing, and sending out seventy disciples to share the Gospel message when Martha and her sister Mary invited Him over for dinner. I imagine Martha had compassion for Jesus because she had heard of how He traveled tirelessly and unselfishly performed good deeds. She was determined to care for this kind man; therefore, she ensured that her home was warm, inviting, hospitable, and refreshing. Martha prepped, cooked, and cleaned, and soon found herself aggravated that her sister Mary had taken an extended break, relaxing at the feet of Jesus. When she could no longer contain her irritation, she asked Jesus to instruct Mary to "get up and help." Jesus gently responded by saying that Mary's choice to "sit and listen" instead of cleaning was more valuable because what she heard was priceless and could not be taken away from her. What an amazing lesson. Can you imagine, Mary would have missed out on a treasured possession if she had not sat to listen and Martha most certainly would have missed out. I imagine as they sat and listened to Jesus, they found rest from the weariness that often comes from simply living.

You and I need that invaluable thing that Jesus mentioned to Martha. I believe it comes by way of simply listening and giving God an opportunity to speak to us. Having all the answers and a strategy is not always necessary. Remember, it is okay to be tired and to stop for rest. A person who lives life well, a well-doer, needs soul rest so she can continue to journey well. The Good Shepherd knows exactly what you need and will lead you down a path that is best if you just listen.

My sheep hear my voice, and I know them, and they follow me. John 10:27 KJV

PRAYER

Heavenly Father,

Thank You for being the Good Shepherd. You are faithful and have promised to care for me. Sheep are wired to listen for the voice of their Shepherd and they find comfort in His guidance. I want to travel this life well, so teach me to listen for Your voice and be still when necessary. In the time of distress, settle my heart, and give me courage as I wait in Your presence. In Jesus' name I pray. Amen.

REFLECTION

1 = Very Bad, 2 = Poor, 3 = Average, 4 = Good, 5 = Excellent

1. Using the scale from 1-5, how well do I sit before God and simply listen?

2. Is there room for improvement?

3. If any, what steps will I take with God toward being a good listener?

~A well-doer listens~

Chapter Two

The Well-Doer
GIVES HERSELF GRACE

I have found that my truest healing happens when I lean into both my strengths and weaknesses. Of course, it is easier to shift my weight toward my strengths because it highlights the good; however, it is a totally different experience pressing into my weaknesses.

I recently heard an interview with a woman who shared her story of falling into a love affair with a co-worker turned mentor. She described her husband as a great guy and her best friend since childhood. They shared three young children together and from the outside looking in, they were the perfect family. Nonetheless, she found herself entangled in a secret love affair for years. The affair was eventually exposed, but after several weeks of being apart, she and her lover resumed their indiscretions. The husband was aware of her relapse, yet resolved that he would not leave his wife, but would selflessly fight for his marriage despite his heart being broken into a million pieces. At this point in the affair, all her friends and relatives were aware of her bad behavior and infidelity. She described herself as rebelliously in love with her mentor, all the while loathing herself, and feeling unworthy of anything good because of her bad behavior.

Still in all, she described this moment in her life as being incredibly freeing. Why? Because she no longer had to sneak, lie, and put on a facade now that she had been totally exposed. Her mistakes, secrets and rebellion were clearly seen by everyone. Strangely enough, this space gifted her with a lighter load and the freedom to see herself plainly for who she was. With the weight of denial and dishonesty removed, she could now see and comprehend the mess she created. When she saw the horror of her behavior, she cried out to the God in whom she always believed, and He answered her. She described this juncture as an "ah hah moment," and scales being removed from her eyes.

What occurred next was a shifting in the deepest part of her soul. She could no longer continue in her adulterous relationship because now she was experiencing the healing and renewing power of the Holy Spirit. Conclusively, the affair ended, she was healed, and her marriage was restored. The journey to renewing the health of her family individually and collectively was an arduous process; however, with love, time, and counsel, they succeeded.

As I listened to her story, I wondered what would have happened if she never arrived at the place where she removed the mask, no longer caring about other people's opinions, and stared herself straight in the face to acknowledge the mess she had created. This was the moment she truly leaned into the bottom line of her destructive and rebellious behavior, which revealed a broken heart in need of healing. You see, what I failed to mention concerning this woman was the fact that she was a Christian, a beloved friend of many, a nurse practitioner by trade, and a CEO of a flourishing business ... the good stuff ... her strengths. Yet, due to a series of compromises, moments of weakness, and I'm sure many other factors, she consequently failed in that particular season of her life. Still, God extended her incredible grace. When she finally cried out to Him, He answered her. As a matter of fact, she noted Him saying to her, "I love and delight in you." I imagine His words were like the soothing touch of a cool breeze on a hot summer day and it was a healing balm to her soul. At this point, she had no other choice but to extend compassion to herself because of the great grace God had given her.

Although I have never found myself in her situation, I consider it an honor to have heard her story and find myself under the tutelage of her experience. Her bravery and strength in sharing her story is honorable. If you and I want to live life well ... to live it healthy, we too must learn to lean into our weaknesses and hardships and call out to God ... transparent and unashamed. Remorseful, yes, but shameful, no. Shame has the tendency to provoke the need to hide and self-loathe. Instead of running to God, we are more inclined to keep our distance from Him because of shame. However, this is the complete opposite of God's heart toward us. The Bible says, "if we confess our sins, He is faithful and just to forgive us our sins, and to cleanse us from all unrighteousness" (1 John 1:9 KJV). The well-doer accepts the truth that God gives grace, remarkable unending grace; therefore, she must extend to herself the same grace and compassion in order to be healed.

10

Leaning into our weaknesses is often the first step on the path that leads to our recovery.

I am reminded of the Apostle John's account of a woman who was caught in adultery. She was unnamed; however, John records that spiteful religious leaders of that time escorted her to Jesus. Their intentions were not pure, but only a test and snare to see if merciful Jesus would uphold the Mosaic law that stated those taken in adultery were to be put to death. The details of this unnamed woman's life are concealed, but let's imagine a scenario for her life. Let's call her Mary. Imagine Mary was beautiful, known throughout her community as generous and cheerful. She loved the outdoors and was often seen picking flowers as she traveled to the open-air communal water trough to wash clothes. There was an innocence about her. She did not participate in the false camaraderie and gossip that often took place at the washing troughs.

Everything about Mary was inviting, and she soon caught the eye of a married man. Let's call him John. John was a respected government official in the local community, married, with two toddler sons. One day he saw Mary in route to the communal water trough; she had stopped to examine a wild crocus flower. The jeweled-toned beauty was captivating, and she had never walked past one without stopping to admire its purple flame on pure white features. John thought it harmless to strike up a conversation with this strikingly beautiful yet ordinary damsel. While talking with Mary, John was intrigued by her simplicity of heart and kind spirit. She thought him to be warm and full of good conversation. John quickly learned Mary frequented this semi-secluded route and ensured he was there to greet and converse with her on most of those days. In the course of time, their affection grew toward one another and their emotional interaction developed into a physical affair. The time they shared together was exciting, exhilarating, full of thorny conviction, and short-lived; they were caught in the act.

It happened so fast, the sound of footsteps, her and John's initial shock, and the men dragging her out of the hideaway into the open court. The commotion was deafening, and her shame was shattering. When they finally hurled her to the ground, she was already broken into a million pieces.

"How did I get here?"

"I knew better."

"This is not who I am. I should have ended it the moment John told me he had a wife and kids."

These were the thoughts that bombarded and swirled around her now guilt-ridden mind.

She would not lift her head for shame. All she heard were the voices telling Jesus several times that she was caught in the act of adultery. They wanted to know His impression on the matter, but He did not reply. Finally, she heard the voice of the man being solicited for an answer. His voice was full of kindness and authority. Jesus was a stranger to her, she had never seen Him before. although she had heard stories about Him, many stories.

Jesus replied, "*Anyone of you who is without sin can throw the first stone.*" Silence, she only heard silence, then the sound of stones dropping to the ground. Lastly, she heard footsteps, many departing footsteps and then again, silence. She sensed Jesus had not moved but she dared not confirm by opening her eyes and lifting her head.

Then He asked, "*Woman, where are your accusers? Did no one accuse you?*"

Mary replied, "*No one, Lord.*"

Jesus replied, "*Neither do I condemn you, go and sin no more.*"

I imagine Mary was astonished and relieved, but more than that, she was loved and felt every bit of it in that moment.

I am inclined to believe Mary took Jesus' admonishment and she sinned no more. You see, something transforming happens in the deepest part of us when Jesus extends grace and we, in turn, gift ourselves with that same grace and compassion. Life can be complicated, and we will stumble along the way. In those moments of stumbling, discouragement, shame, and condemnation await us, but it is vital that we understand God has given us unmerited favor, grace. Jesus paid the penalty of our sins and forever offers us forgiveness and restoration. If you and I are to be well-doers and navigate life well, we must give ourselves the same grace Jesus extends to us. The sooner we adopt this principle, the closer we are to hearing God say, *"Well done, good and faithful servant."*

PRAYER

Dear Heavenly Father,

Thank You for the unmerited favor You have given me through Jesus Christ Your Son. Each time I fall short of what is best for me, Your love and forgiveness await to restore me. Give me courage to lean into my weaknesses and converse with You so that I can be made better. Your mercy is forever and Your compassion is endless; therefore, I will forever run to You. I will extend to myself the same grace You extend to me. Thank You for Your grace. In Jesus' name I pray. Amen.

REFLECTION

1. What does the word grace mean to me?

2. How well do I extend grace to myself?

3. Do I consult God about the area(s) that invokes the need for grace? Why or why not?

4. Are there areas in my life where I have withheld grace?

5. If you answered "yes" to question 4; I encourage you to revisit those areas for wholeness to take place.

Chapter Three

The Well-Doer
REMEMBERS

One day, my husband and I were having Bible study with our three children, ages eleven, twelve, and seventeen. My husband opened the study by talking about Christ's sacrifice for mankind and how God has given us free will to serve Him. This particular topic was not a new subject for our children, for we had discussed it many times over. This time, however, the subject took an unexpected turn, and quickly. I think Jeremy and I both felt an unspoken urgency to talk to the kids about the reality of heaven and hell. I recall sharing with them how I believed I would see all of my deceased loved ones who had gone on before us, like Grandma Loretta, Great-grandma Lucetta, and the twins I

17

miscarried before Joshua and Caleb were born—and what do you know, out gushed the waterworks! The kids were mesmerized as we talked of heaven and the reality of hell. You could hear a pin drop.

We continued by cautioning them they would undoubtedly, someday, encounter people and circumstances that would solicit them to doubt their faith. In those moments, we explained how important it is for them to remember who God has been to them and who He is in their hearts. My children are all miracles in one way or another and they are keenly aware of the fact. Not only that, they have had the privilege of experiencing God's presence for themselves.

For this reason, *"Madison, Joshua, and Caleb, you must have the courage to stand up for God. If your faith is ever challenged, simply remember what He has done for you...this is your testimony, your evidence. Be courageous."*

I went on to share with them about an experience I had in the eighth grade. I attended Richard J. Oglesby Elementary School, located on the Southside of Chicago. I remember it was springtime, the classroom windows were open, and the sun shined brightly in our science class. The kids were rowdy, full of energy and life. It probably was nearing the end of the school day because I recall the scent of sheer happiness being in the atmosphere. Somehow, the class began an open and guided discussion about God and His existence. There was a strong consensus swirling that God was not real.

The shyness in me took a backseat and an irresistible boldness compelled me to my feet to make the case for God. Earlier that year, I spent the weekend at my cousin Jennifer's house. Jenny was my best friend and we would stay up all night yapping until I fell asleep; I was always the first to crash. Hours later, in the wee hours of the morning, Jenny awakened, frightened by a nightmare that a burglar had broken into the house. She immediately woke me up. We, being young, gullible, and terrified went into the kitchen, secured a knife, and went back to bed.

A short while later, we were awakened by my Aunt Valerie screaming, "Jenny! Jenny! Call 911!"

Dazed, we ran to the living room to witness my aunt frantically holding the window down on the leg of a burglar. He was trying to break into the house! The screams and commotion eventually scared him away. The police arrived later and proceeded to close out a bizarre and terrifying experience.

Jennifer and I, while scared, held the testimony that God forewarned us in a dream of the attempted burglary.

So, as I stood before my class, I boldly testified of God's existence because I remembered how He revealed Himself to Jennifer and me. I didn't need affirmation, nor did I await a popular vote, because I remembered what He had done for me personally. In the same spirit, my husband and I implored our children.

I gracefully caution you that you will encounter circumstances that are contrary to God's existence and power in your life. Everything in you may feel compelled to doubt God, but do not doubt, only believe, and remember His faithfulness and promises to you. Remembering is crucial to you being a well-doer.

I am reminded of Jochebed, the mother of Moses. A woman whose life canvas was richly colorful. History reports that she was the daughter of Levi. Levi being one of the twelve sons of Jacob. She was a descendent of Abraham, the father and hero of faith. Surely, she was raised from childhood hearing family stories of the great exploits carried out by the God of her ancestors. She was a woman of faith.

I imagine, the morning of Moses' birth was like no other. The sunlit room was warmed by a peace that seemed unnatural. The typical suffocation felt in the air was suspended and freedom seemed to sway like a flag moved by a soft breeze. The weight of the Egyptian oppression never seemed to lift, and the recent decree issued by Pharaoh, to toss every newborn Hebrew boy in the Nile River was viciously crushing; yet, in this moment none of that mattered. Moses was beautiful, unusually beautiful. The moment Jochebed set eyes on him, she knew his destiny was not at the bottom of the Nile River; he was not born just to die. He would live ... she would see to it.

Each day following his birth was filled with both exhilarating joy and excruciating pain. The plan she set in motion wasn't quite complete; she simply lived in the moment and resolved to care for and love him each day as if it were her last. In between the love and care, she would hide him and quiet his every sound to conceal his presence from the Egyptian soldiers who patrolled just outside her quarters. Moses was growing and now responding to the sound of Jochebed's voice by smiling, squirming, cooing, and making gurgling sounds. This was when she experienced joy and pain simultaneously, because while his beautiful growth gave her joy, it also made him more vulnerable to being discovered. Jochebed knew that she couldn't hide Moses for much longer.

As she lay awake one night, sleep escaping her once again, she began to recall the stories of victory wrought by the God of her ancestors. She remembered how her dad Levi would tell her about her Great-Great Grandfather Abraham who once was ordered by God to offer his son Isaac as a burnt offering upon a mountain. Isaac wasn't just his son, but he was Abraham's beloved and miracle child. Isaac was born when Abraham was 100 years old and Sarah, his mother, was 90 years old. God's command was real, and the death of Isaac had to be unfathomable; yet Abraham never envisioned his death but believed God would make a way and provide Himself a sacrifice in place of Isaac.

In this moment, Jochebed's heart reminded her that if God made a way of escape for Isaac, surely He could and would make a way for Moses to live.

My dear friend, Jochebed didn't forget God's history and track record in her lineage. She remembered. When times were tough, she reached back and found the proof that God worked miracles, and if He did it once before, then He could do it again. You see, a well-doer is not easily hopeless, but knows how to pull on faith, even if she has to reach back in her memory bank and recall God's track record in her life. If you and I live long enough, life will present us with bleak and often hopeless circumstances. Like Jochebed, we cannot afford to forget, but must remember the God in whom we believe.

Jochebed constructed a plan that may have seemed foolish to the naked eye, but she was seeing through the lenses of faith. By faith, she built a basket made from a tall rush-like water plant. She covered the basket with tar and pitch to make it waterproof. She put her baby boy in the basket and placed it in the reeds of the Nile. I imagine as she was building the basket and when she finally placed Moses in the river, that she prayed ferociously, and she reminded God of His past miracles and her present faith in Him. You see, her plan was not haphazard, but it was peppered with prayer and faith, provoked by the simple memory of God's faithfulness. She literally arrested the nagging thought that said she was mad, and out of her mind for attempting such a feat. By the time she placed her infant son in the Nile, her heart was fixed and not afraid. Faith and prayer does that. The unseen force of prayer can make even the desperate heart of a mother who is in dire straits be at peace.

Can you imagine what would have become of Moses if Jochebed had not reached back and remembered the testimonies of her lineage? When baby Moses was placed in the Nile River, he was found by the daughter of the most powerful person in Egypt, Pharaoh. When she found him, she immediately took him in as her own son and allowed his mother Jochebed, unbeknownst to her, to breastfeed and care for him. In the eyes of Pharaoh's daughter, Jochebed was just another enslaved Hebrew available to meet her needs and that was to care for her newly found precious baby boy. However, Jochebed was far from that, she was a woman whose faith had penetrated heaven and moved the favor of God to work on her behalf. You see, the river that harbored the dead bodies of possibly hundreds of Hebrew babies was Moses' path to life and not death.

A well-doer, like Jochebed, will always remember God's faithfulness. Remembering and trusting in God is not always easy. I believe if you and I, like Jochebed, would only believe, moving according to the faith in our hearts and not the circumstances of the moment, then we too will find victory and light on the other side.

On a winter day in 2015, I paid a visit to my rheumatologist because I had not been feeling well physically. I was experiencing unusual tiredness, weakness, and fatigue. The trip to the rheumatology clinic was over an hour away from my home. Upon arrival and after a physical examination, my doctor determined that lab work was required in order to make an informed decision about my current health and symptoms. The lab results would take hours to come back, therefore, my doctor sent me home with instructions to rest and to keep a close eye on my symptoms, with the reassurance he would call me if my results were concerning. As I traveled home, I decided to pick up fast food for dinner because the hour was late, and I would not get home in time to cook dinner for the family. When I arrived home, I greeted my family and began unpacking the food. Then I received a call from my rheumatology nurse, instructing me to return to the hospital for admission because my platelets were dangerously low. Consequently, I informed my family and packed my bags for what I knew would be a prolonged hospital stay.

You see, nearly a year prior to the date, I was diagnosed with Thrombotic Thrombocytopenic Purpura (TTP) subsequent to Systemic Lupus Erythematosus. TTP is a rare blood disorder that causes blood clots to form in the small blood vessels throughout the body. The clots can limit or block the flow of oxygen-rich blood to the body's vital organs, such as the brain, kidneys, and heart. The low platelets found on my lab results were the result of the TTP. Due to the diagnosis the year prior and current lab results, my doctor quickly recognized the symptoms and knew the necessary treatment plan.

As a result, I was now diagnosed with severe TTP because I had relapsed within a year's time from the initial diagnosis. The treatment and hospital experience the year prior was brutal and extensive, and included two weeks of blood transfusions, daily plasma exchanges, and poking and prodding from an exceptional team of specialists. During that experience, God stayed by my side, comforted and strengthened me, and most importantly, He miraculously healed me.

Fast forward a year later. When I received the phone call from my doctor's office instructing me to return to the hospital for admission, my heart was not afraid. As I traveled back to the hospital, I cried out to the Lord and made a simple request: I asked Him to give me courage and make my heart strong. The memory of how He miraculously healed me the year prior and how He showed His kindness toward me during that experience was ingrafted in my mind. I remembered and trusted His healing power, but what I needed from Him in the present hour was courage and a strong heart because I knew from experience the extensive treatment that lay ahead could easily provoke fear in my heart.

I was in the hospital for one week this time around and recovered much quicker. I was able to approach a scary situation with faith and not fear, because I remembered what God had done for me the year prior.

My dear sister, hide in the deepest part of your heart the knowledge that a well-doer never forgets, but remembers the faithfulness of her God.

PRAYER

Dear Heavenly Father,

Thank You for the gift of memory. You have given me a memory bank from which I can always withdraw testaments of Your faithfulness, not only toward me, but unto all generations. You are always good and will never change. I will always remember Your goodness and promises. If I were to ever forget, even if but for a moment, Holy Spirit, quickly remind me. I desire to live life well and always remember Your wondrous works. Thank You for hearing me. In Jesus' name. Amen.

REFLECTION

1. Take a moment to reminisce and recall seven notable things God has done for you. Write them down on the following pages provided.

2. Starting on a Monday, for seven days, talk to God through prayer and thank Him for one thing on your list each day.

3. For seven days, tell someone about one thing on your list.

Monday

I remember when:

_____

_____

_____

_____

_____

_____

_____

_____

_____

I will share my testimony with:

_____

_____

_____

_____

Tuesday

I remember when:

_____

_____

_____

_____

_____

_____

_____

_____

_____

_____

I will share my testimony with:

_____

_____

_____

_____

Wednesday

I remember when:

_____

_____

_____

_____

_____

_____

_____

_____

_____

_____

I will share my testimony with:

_____

_____

_____

_____

Thursday

I remember when:

_____

_____

_____

_____

_____

_____

_____

_____

_____

_____

I will share my testimony with:

_____

_____

_____

Friday

I remember when:

_____

_____

_____

_____

_____

_____

_____

_____

_____

_____

I will share my testimony with:

_____

_____

_____

Saturday

I remember when:

_____

_____

_____

_____

_____

_____

_____

_____

_____

_____

I will share my testimony with:

_____

_____

_____

_____

Sunday

I remember when:

_____

_____

_____

_____

_____

_____

_____

_____

_____

I will share my testimony with:

_____

_____

_____

_____

Chapter Four

The Well-Doer
DOES WHAT IS RIGHT

I surrendered my life to Christ at the tender age of fifteen. During my sophomore year of high school, my mother relocated my two brothers and me from Chicago, Illinois, to a small town just two hours away from the city. She was determined to save us from the violence and statistics that all too often victimized African-American kids who grew up on the south side of Chicago. Relocation was her way of saving us. Unfortunately, I did not take the move very well because family and friends whom I loved were left behind. In addition, we moved from a bustling city to a quiet town where the culture was entirely foreign to me. Needless to say, I became an angry middle child who sadly did not have the capacity to understand the wisdom and love in my mother's decision to relocate. Months after our move, I found myself expressing my displeasure in life to my cousin Jenny over the phone. I absolutely adored her and knew I could tell her anything and she would understand.

During this particular phone call, her response to my venting and woes was unusually different. She did not jump on the band wagon of my complaint, but began telling me about the goodness of Jesus and how He could repair my broken heart. Jenny encouraged me to fall on my knees and ask Jesus to come into my heart. After our phone call, that was exactly what I did. I went to my bedroom, fell on my knees, and asked the Lord to come into my heart and help me and "boy oh boy," did He answer my prayer! From that day forward, my life was forever changed. I no longer thought, conversed, or behaved the same prior to my encounter with Jesus.

During my senior year of high school, I decided that I wanted to join the United States Air Force. My mother agreed it would be a great experience, therefore, shortly after my high school graduation, I was off to basic training in San Antonio, Texas. I remember the enormous support I received from my church family and the prayers offered for me prior to my departure, but what stands out most is the promise the Lord spoke to my heart. He promised He would be with me through all my paths of life. I remember reading the following passage of scripture and hiding it deep within my soul:

> *My child do not forget my teaching, but let your heart keep my commandments, for they will provide a long and full life, and well-being for you. Do not let mercy and truth leave you; bind them around your neck, write them on the tablet of your heart. Then you will find favor and good understanding, in the sight of God and people. Proverbs 3:1-4 New English Translation*

I held tightly to this promise and endeavored to hold fast to God's principles, and to simply do what was right. Approximately five months after departing for basic military training in Texas, I arrived at my first duty station in England. My time in England was monumental in that I met and married the love of my life, Jeremy, at the tender age of nineteen, and forged lifelong friendships that still flourish to this day.

A typical military couple, Jeremy and I found ourselves journeying across the world to various states and countries, most times together, sometimes apart, in honor of our service commitment to our country. Our life together has truly been good, but not without challenges and uncertainties. Add the element of children and the hustle and bustle of life to the equation, and you can imagine what life looked like, at times, for us. Life was, and is, ever evolving, both naturally and figuratively.

Jeremy and I determined, very early in our marriage, whenever we encountered seasons of uncertainty and found ourselves unsure of the correct path to take, we would always choose to do what was right. We adopted the principle, *"If you do not know what do, simply follow what is right."* There are several passages in the Bible that highlight this life-anchoring principle:

> *The integrity of the upright shall guide them: but the perverseness of transgressors shall destroy them. Proverbs 11:3 KJV*

The righteousness of the perfect shall direct his way: but the wicked shall fall by his own wickedness. Proverbs 11:5 KJV

You see, these passages highlight the truth that walking in integrity and doing what is right will act as a compass for your life. I can humbly say that Jeremy and I have had a good life because we have endeavored to live by this principle, and therefore have reaped the benefit of never being lost, without hope and an answer. Remember the passage I mentioned earlier in the chapter:

My child do not forget my teaching, but let your heart keep my commandments, for they will provide a long and full life, and well-being for you. Proverbs 3:1-2 New English Translation

The phrase *'you can take it to the bank'* definitely applies to this proven promise. My husband and I are living witnesses to the benefits of adhering to it.

I am reminded of Abigail, whom the Bible describes as a wise and beautiful woman. She was married to a wealthy, yet foolish man named Nabal. As a matter of fact, he was described as cruel and mean. I initially wondered why a woman of Abigail's stature would join herself to such a man, but I was quickly reminded that marriages in Bible times were not created for love, per se, but for the joint interest of both families involved. Jewish marriages were generally arranged by the fathers of the bride and groom and began with a betrothal, or engagement. The bride's and groom's feelings on the marriage were seldom taken into consideration, and it was probable that the bride and groom had never met before the engagement. Be that as it may, Abigail found herself married to a cruel man, yet I believe she remained honorable and unaltered in character despite Nabal's callous and often merciless behavior. I imagine she was governed by integrity and was fixed on honoring her father's name and her marital commitment. Why else would the Bible, upon introduction, immediately describe her as a woman of "good understanding"? This undoubtedly was a dominant character trait she possessed. I suppose there were days that Nabal's foolishness and cruelty vexed her soul. Yet, instead of responding according to his foolery, which often translated into irresponsibility, Abigail behaved wisely and remained faithful to the principles that governed her heart.

Such as the occasion when David and his men were doing their normal business and found themselves lurking in the Carmel deserts. Coincidentally, Nabal's shepherds were there too. During this time, Philistine raids were very common, and shepherds were vulnerable to their onslaught. However, David and his men were kind to Nabal's shepherds and served as protection to them and their flocks. So later, when David and his men found themselves in need of victuals and heard that Nabal's shepherds were shearing sheep, he sent ten young men to Nabal to request his generosity.

Through his messengers, David introduced himself, informed Nabal of the kindness he had shown his shepherds while in the desert, and humbly requested victuals for him and his men. True to his character, Nabal's response was harsh and cruel. This was a foolish response on Nabal's part because he immediately made himself David's enemy, and in that moment, David had determined to kill Nabal and everyone associated with him.

One of Nabal's servants overheard the exchange between David's men and Nabal and was instantly troubled, for he knew the fate that was to befall Nabal at the hand of David. Hands sweating and heart racing, the servant ran to Abigail's chamber to inform her of the exchange and impending doom. Initially unsure of what to do or how to respond, Abigail retreated to following the integrity of her heart. She did not support her husband's behavior; therefore, in her mind, the solution was not to forewarn him, so he could go into hiding or even worse, exasperate matters. Doing the right thing was her only option, which entailed having her servant saddle her donkey, prepare victuals, and right the wrong of her husband's cruel response to David. She would grant David's request herself. According to ancient traditions, sheep shearing time was a time of extravagant hospitality towards others, and there was always enough food and plenty to spare. Abigail was determined that the generosity of this season would be no different, especially since David had declared war on Nabal's stinginess.

Abigail sent her servants before her to meet David while she followed close behind. Upon seeing David, she jumped off her saddle and humbled herself before him. She recounted her husband's malice toward him and pleaded for Nabal's pardon, exclaiming that he was a foolish man. She gently offered victuals to him and his men. Most notably, she reminded David that he was highly favored of the Lord, with a divine future ahead of him, and avenging himself against a man of Nabal's character was beneath him and opposite of God's best for him. David was pleased with Abigail's efforts and wisdom; therefore, he blessed and honored her request.

Sadly, when Abigail shared with Nabal the fate that would have befallen him at the hand of David, barring her intervention, the Bible says he fell dead ten days afterward. I presume he was overwhelmed at the mere thought of what would have taken place. Abigail, on the other hand, was now a free woman and became the wife of one of the greatest kings to ever live, David. Her decision to live by integrity and do what was right changed her future for good. You see, it is highly possible that Abigail's marriage to Nabal was arranged and not her choosing; yet, because she was a woman of understanding and wisdom, the Lord did not forget her. The path of righteousness led her out of the arms of a cruel and foolish man, and into the arms of a man with the reputation of being one after God's own heart. Her integrity uprooted her from cruelty and planted her in love. Remember the Bible says, *"the righteousness of the upright delivers them"* (Pr. 11:6 NIV), and Abigail was surely delivered.

My friend, I encourage you to always allow integrity to lead you. In times of uncertainty, follow what is right and it will act as a compass and lead you in the direction you should go. This is the practice of the well-doer.

PRAYER

Dear Heavenly Father,

Thank You for Your righteousness, for You are the ultimate path that leads us to safety. I pray that You will give me the courage and strength to always follow what is right, because that path will lead me to Your will. Help me to cherish Your statutes and precepts, for therein will I find the abundance of life. Thank You for answering my prayers. In Jesus' name. Amen.

REFLECTION

1. Is there an area in your life where you struggle to do what is right? If yes, explain why?

2. Consider taking three consecutive days to pray specifically about this area, for at least three to five minutes.

3. Ask the Lord to fill your heart with honor, and a divine desire to please Him above all. If you do this, I assure you the Lord will begin to transform your heart.

Chapter Five

The Well-Doer
LIVES WITH ETERNITY IN MIND

And as it is appointed unto men once to die, but
after this the judgment. Hebrews 9:27 KJV

Since I was a young girl, I have always been keenly aware of life and death, especially the brevity of the human life. When I was three to five years old, I would climb onto my grandmother's bathroom sink and stare into the mirror. I would study every crevasse of the rich, dark countenance staring back at me: my slanted eyes, full lips, and dark eyebrows. I could not get away from my eyes, because they seemed to hold a story, as if they possessed secrets they were eager to tell. Staring into the mirror, I would often ask myself, *"Who are you, or for that matter, what are you?"* This went on for as long as I can remember. Moments like these instilled in me an awareness that there was more to life, and more to my existence, than what was visible to the naked eye.

I believe those were moments where God, the Creator of life, was making Himself acquainted with me, even without my knowing. When I looked into the mirror and beheld my eyes, I saw a glimpse of the eternity that resided in the deepest part of me. I'm sure you've had similar experiences in your life at some point or the other; I'm convinced we all have. If our lives were a crime scene, examined by an investigator who intricately dusted the crime area for fingerprints, he would find the oil from God's fingerprints on almost every inch of our lives.

I must be honest, I do not possess complete understanding as to why God created mankind, although I have my theories, based on biblical research. I do know mankind is on a pilgrimage through this life and this earth is not our final destination. If earth were our home, physical death would not exist, but it does...we die. Jesus was very clear when the day of His crucifixion drew near, and He and His disciples had finished their last supper together. As they gathered, I imagine the atmosphere and mood was somber as Jesus told the disciples that He was departing this world and going back to the Father. The disciples had questions and were uneasy, but Jesus provided comfort by reassuring them they would someday join Him. He was going away to prepare a place for them. A place with many mansions. Again, confirming earth is not the final destination.

Due to life's brevity and in the interest of time, it is important that you and I govern our lives with eternity in mind. In the book's introduction, I mentioned how I was intrigued by the lives of many great people who once made earth their home, but are no longer with us. They were born, roamed the territory allotted to them, may or may not have discovered and utilized their God-given gifts, and some even raised families. In the space between birth and death, there were many choices, roads, and experiences afforded to them. *How did they choose? Did they choose well? Did the path they chose lead toward God? Was God pleased with those choices?* You see, God gives life opportunity to us all. He desires that we live to the fullest while keeping one thing in mind...Him. King Solomon, in his God-given wisdom, after sitting under the tutelage of life and writing his dissertation, concluded that man ought to fear God, and keep His commandments: for this is his whole duty and, in the end, God will judge our work, whether good or bad, and most certainly without our permission.

Dr. Martin Luther King, Jr., was a Christian minister and a strong leader and activist from the mid-1950s until his assassination in 1968. He pursued equality and civil rights for African-Americans and all victims of injustice. The opposition to his efforts was tremendous. He encountered many threats and his physical life was in constant danger. During his most famous speech, Dr. King expressed courage and affirmed that he was not afraid to die. As a matter of fact, longevity was not his aim, but only seeing the vision of equality come to pass. Dr. King had a mission from God and his life's movement was according to God's plan for him. His choice was to live with eternity in mind. Despite life's difficulties, Dr. King never lost sight of his mission nor his God, as expressed in his speech below:

> *Well, I don't know what will happen now. We've got some difficult days ahead. But it really doesn't matter with me now, because I've been to the*

mountaintop. And I don't mind. Like anybody, I would like to live – a long life; longevity has its place. But I'm not concerned about that now. I just want to do God's will. And He's allowed me to go up to the mountain. And I've looked over. And I've seen the Promised Land. I may not get there with you. But I want you to know tonight, that we, as a people, will get to the Promised Land. So, I'm happy, tonight. I'm not worried about anything. I'm not fearing any man. Mine eyes have seen the glory of the coming of the Lord (Eidenmuller, 2001-Present).

I regard Dr. Martin Luther King Jr., as a well-doer. He went about doing good and he lived life well. Do you remember the woman described in the Bible as the virtuous woman (Proverbs 31)? I believe she, too, was a well-doer who lived with eternity in mind. She lived life so well, her description earned her the right to be written in the Bible for generations following to read. She nurtured her family. She was a caring wife whose husband fully trusted her, and her children called her blessed. She was charitable and helped the poor. She was described as a woman of wisdom and kindness. Most importantly, she was strong...clothed with strength, and undisturbed by the winds of life, because she feared the Lord.

Like the *virtuous woman*, a well-doer gives every effort to live life well and lives with eternity in mind. Life on earth expires quickly, but eternity is forever. Our departure from this life to the next will arrive sooner rather than later. Friend, enjoy this gift God has given you, pursue your purpose, and remember to live with eternity in mind.

> *Behold, what I have seen to be good and fitting is to eat and drink and find enjoyment in all the toil with which one toils under the sun the few days of his life that God has given him, for this is his lot. Ecclesiastes 5:18 ERV*

> *Rejoice, O young man, in your youth, and let your heart cheer you in the days of your youth. Walk in the ways of your heart and the sight of your eyes. But know that for all these things God will bring you into judgment. Ecclesiastes 11:9 ERV*

PRAYER

Heavenly Father,

Thank You for giving me a life to live, explore, and enjoy. Help me to live my life to the fullest. Open my eyes to see the beauty and opportunities You have created just for me, and give me courage to pursue them. Most importantly, may I remember You all the days of my life and live with eternity in mind. In Jesus' name I pray. Amen.

REFLECTION

1. What does "living with eternity in mind" mean to you?

2. God desires for you to enjoy your life; it is His gift to you. Are you intentional in enjoying your life? Why or why not?

3. In what ways can you better enjoy life and live with eternity in mind?

Chapter Six

The Well-Doer
REMAINS TENDER

Tenderhearted

-ADJECTIVE

having a compassionate, kindly, or sensitive disposition.
(American Heritage Dictionary of the English Language, 2016)

I remember being a young, excited, nineteen-year-old new-lywed. I was having the time of my life with my husband Jeremy, and the friends we had acquired while stationed at Royal Air Force Lakenheath in Suffolk, England, serving in the United States Air Force. During that time, I was a Medical Services Administration technician and provided critical support to a healthcare team by preparing patients for aeromedical evacuations between Europe and the United States. My job was incredibly rewarding because, along with my team, I had the opportunity to serve and comfort people who were often in the midst of a health crisis.

One of my responsibilities involved arranging transportation and lodging for incoming patients. I would accompany the transportation unit to the flight line (military airport) to pick up the patients and then ensure the patients were dropped off at their appropriate lodging facility, whether that was the hotel on a military installation or the inpatient ward at the base hospital. My heart was very empathetic toward these patients and I made every effort to serve them with kindness. On one occasion, I went so far as to invite a young female patient who was a navy sailor to stay overnight at my house, because lodging was unavailable. In addition to health challenges, this young lady was also facing a host of other arduous personal circumstances. That evening at my house was spent talking life and God. We prayed, cried together, and she even rededicated her life to Christ. Life for me was a field full of birds, butterflies, and sweetly scented tulips. I was young, optimistic, with a tender heart.

My supervisor at the time was a Christian woman who was outspoken and very direct. She loved the Lord, but often came off brash because she pulled no punches. She was enlisted, and it secretly tickled me that her personality intimated both superior officers and subordinates alike. I've literally seen superior officers leave her presence shaking in their boots. Notwithstanding, she was sweet when you got to know her, and personally she left a positive impact on my life. One of the biggest imprints she left on my heart happened when she and I had a conversation about an encounter I thought she mishandled, as a Christian. The encounter was not unethical, but I thought she was unnecessarily tactless and harsh.

Her response to my concern was, "*Tikita, I have not always been this way. People and life made me this way.*"

I must admit, being a young Christian and not having lived much life at that time, I disdained her statement. It wasn't until years later, after I "lived a little," encountered difficult people, and experienced disappointments, that I finally understood and empathized with her point of view.

Over a decade later, I found myself in conflict with a different supervisor. By nature, I am pretty long-suffering and accommodating, but on this particular day my supervisor's condescending tone was insulting and patronizing and I let her know that I would not tolerate it. During my lunch break, I called my very straightforward, no nonsense grandmother, and spewed my complaint onto her listening ears. I was on a verbal rampage, telling my grandmother how I set my supervisor straight, and how my supervisor failed to realize she was dealing with a "full-grown" woman. My grandmother was unusually silent on the other end and allowed me to express my offense.

When I finally finished, she said, "*Tikita baby, stay tender. Do not allow people to make you hard; remain sweet.*"

I was slightly surprised by my grandmother's comment, because she was one who commanded respect and did not hesitate to confront those who withheld it. On the other hand, since I was a little girl, she would always tell me I was special and how God had a special plan for me. She believed my mild-mannered personality was a gift from God. I believe when she listened to my complaint that afternoon, she immediately recognized that my defensive disposition was not part of God's special plan for me, it was a threat. She had lived enough life to recognize the signs of a tender heart becoming bitter and calloused due to the blows of life. My grandmother's words humbled me, and most importantly, reminded me that God's desire for me was not to be overcome by bad behavior, but to overcome bad behavior with good. The Bible says, "*The way of the righteous is like the first gleam of dawn, which shines ever brighter until the full light of day.*" *Proverbs 4:18 NLT*

As we follow the way of Jesus, we get better and our light shines brighter. We must be intentional to guard our hearts and navigate life in a manner that warrants God's blessing and coveted words of, "Well done." Friend, endeavor to remain tender in heart and do not become hardened by the winds of life.

I am reminded of Job's wife. She was a mother of seven sons and three daughters and was married to one of the wealthiest men in the area. Life was good. Her husband was an honorable man, well respected, and her children were happy. Unfortunately, tragedy struck her family. She and Job lost their fortune and unimaginably, all ten of their children died in a freak accident. To add insult to injury, Job fell gravely ill. I must admit, I cannot begin to imagine the level of grief and darkness Job and his wife felt. After the simultaneous death of all their children, the only logical response in my mind would be to literally drop dead from grief. But no, Job and his wife's grief did not result in death by heartache.

Job grieved on a large scale but remained honorable in his temperament. Job's wife, on the other hand, was broken and aggravated at the notion that he maintained his integrity under such tragic circumstances. Not only did Job lose his wealth and children, he was now gravely ill. Yet, he never faltered in his reverence toward God; his heart remained tender.

One day, disgusted by Job's countercultural behavior, his wife scornfully said to him, "*Do you still maintain your integrity? Curse God and die.*"

Job's response was, "*You talk like a foolish woman. Shall we accept only good from the hand of God?*"

Whoa! The condition of Job's heart is one to be coveted.

To Job's wife's defense, I imagine she felt hollow and lost, as did Job. The difference between the two of them was the postures of their hearts. My husband Jeremy's and my life motto is, "*When you don't know what to do or where to turn, then do what is right,*" for it will lead you down the path that is best. Personally, I have never experienced pain on a scale like Job and his wife, so I cannot positively say that under the same circumstances I would choose to remain humble and tender before the Lord. On the contrary, I do know Job chose to maintain a tender heart and it led him to a place of understanding, healing, and ultimately, a life better than the one he lived prior to when tragedy struck.

I have racked my brain and inquired of the Lord why Job's wife's heart posture was drastically different from his. Consequently, the only explanation that came to mind is the fact Job's intimate and consistent relationship with God made the difference in his perspective and response. In the Bible's introduction of Job, it explains that he feared God, shunned evil, and sanctified and interceded for his children daily. Job feared God, yes, but most importantly, I imagine he intentionally set aside time to be with God ... daily. Do you know a close relationship with God literally transforms you? His presence is wonderful; it changes you, oftentimes without your awareness. God's great light illuminates everything about you, to include the way you perceive this temporary life and the circumstances that come along with it.

The well-doer maintains a tender heart under the hardest of circumstances because of the transforming power that comes from close, consistent, and intentional relationship with God. Will you endeavor to remain delicate and tender-hearted despite life's circumstances and encounters? Friend, allow the light of Jesus to shine brighter in your heart with each passing day. In this, God is well pleased.

> *The way of the righteous is like the first gleam of dawn, which shines ever brighter until the full light of day. Proverbs 4:18 NLT*

PRAYER

Heavenly Father,

The Bible instructs us to guard our hearts with all diligence because from it flows the issues of life. Our heart has the ability to influence every aspect of our lives. Help me to remain tender and humble before You. May I always have a heart of flesh and not of stone; do not allow me to be hardened by people, life circumstances, or cultural influences. Thank You for hearing and answering my prayer. In Jesus' name I pray. Amen

REFLECTION

1. Is protecting the posture of your heart important to you? Why or why not?

2. How often do you talk to God about your heart?

3. Do you forgive well?

4. What are some practical steps you can take toward maintaining a tender heart?

Chapter Seven

The Well-Doer
PRAYS

"She Laughs At Her Future"

"Mom, are you worried about the boys? I mean, their future and all?"

This was a question posed by my then sixteen-year-old daughter, Madison.

I laughed and replied, "No baby, I'm not worried at all."

She was in the thick of feeling the weight of what it is to love someone beyond yourself, so much so that it propels you to attempt to peep into their future and often results in a ton of scenarios playing in your head. Madison had grown to truly love her younger siblings, Joshua and Caleb, who were nine and ten years old at the time. She had lived enough life to understand that the world outside of our home was not always pretty, and even more, she understood the gravity of good and bad choices. She wondered if her brothers would choose wisely, and the mere possibilities of their decisions troubled her.

I empathized with her in that moment because I remembered there were times when the thought of her future paralyzed every fiber of my heart with fear, especially her freshman year of high school. Madison, my firstborn, has always been the absolute joy of my life, and the thought of trouble in her present or future troubled me.

As a military family, we relocated often, usually every three to four years. In Madison's freshman year of high school, we found ourselves in the Washington, D.C. Metropolitan Area, in the state of Maryland. While we lived in an upper middle-class community, the children within the community were very mature and often lived life well beyond what their ages should have allowed. Madison, on the other hand, was "green" compared to them and lived a significant portion of her childhood in Oklahoma. The cultural differences between the two states were immense. That year, Madison developed significant anxiety and was faced with peer pressure on every-side. I knew that year would be defining and would yield an impact that would affect the cadence of the years to follow. In essence, it would leave an imprint on the core of who she was and who she was to become.

Interestingly enough, the summer prior to her freshman year, I was in the thick of marketing and promoting my inaugural book, *Undisturbed*, including speaking engagements and book signings. However, at the start of the school year, I purposed in my heart to redirect my focus and energy from the book to Madison. During this time, I recall receiving several phone calls inquiring about book promotion activities and I would frankly respond that I had put my book on the shelf in order to focus on Madison during this pivotal stage of her life. As a result, I submerged myself in her school system by joining the PTA, volunteering, and simply being present. I knew everyone on her cheerleading team, followed practically the entire student body on Twitter, knew who was dating whom, all to gain the pulse of the children who were a part of my child's school culture. Thankfully, Madison didn't mind. She thought it was pretty cool that I was in the know, especially when she had "tea to spill," as she called it. Still, deep in my heart, I knew my practical efforts were not enough because the great majority of the battle my child faced was spiritual, which she was neither equipped nor skilled enough to fight. Prayer was my answer and I had to suspend all I knew about it and ask God to teach me again to pray, strategically and for this moment in time. Boy oh boy, did He answer my prayer and take me on what seemed like a prayer boot camp journey ... a glorious journey!

My prayer journey began by getting up Monday through Friday, anywhere between 2:30 and 5 a.m. in the morning. I would leave my bedroom to go to my living room, screened-in back porch, or my basement. During the day, the Lord would lead me to Bible Scriptures to pray during the night. For instance, the Bible describes Jesus as the Branch of Jesse. It expresses how the Spirit of the Lord would make Him of quick understanding and declares He would not judge by His sight nor reprove by what He heard.

> *And shall make him of quick understanding in the fear of the Lord: and he shall not judge after the sight of his eyes, neither reprove after the hearing of his ears: Isaiah 11:3 KJV*

Well, Madison was dealing with immense peer pressure and encountered thought patterns and ideologies that were contrary to her home values, much like many teenagers. Unfortunately, I could not make her choose what to believe, but only talk her through what I believed to be true according to God's statutes and principles. The choice was hers; it was a part of growing up. However, I possessed massive power through the spirit of prayer. I began praying Isaiah 11:3 over Madison. I asked the Lord to give her quick understanding; to help her to discern between good and evil, clean and unclean, and holy and vile. In addition, I asked Him to give her the will and ability to choose what is right. In essence, I prayed that she would possess divine discernment that she might see things for what they truly were. As a result, the most incredible thing happened during Madison's freshman year and over the course of her high school career. I saw my prayers being manifested in her behavior. It was so wonderful to witness my daughter maintaining a tender heart in the midst of a challenging and soliciting environment.

As a parent, I did not leave her heart to chance, but strategically prayed daily that the Lord would give her a heart of flesh and not of stone. As I write this, Madison just graduated from high school, and I often describe her as having a sweet, tender heart. It is the highlight of her character. She's kind, empathetic, and has a heart for human justice. I know the posture of her heart is simply a result of my husband and I praying strategically for areas of concern.

Throughout this prayer journey, there were times that I placed pictures of Madison on my living room floor, turned on worship music, and danced before the Lord around her picture. As I danced, I believe grace was released toward her. Grace, as described by my good friend, Lowray Bartney, is God's supernatural power on and in her, to do what she could not do herself. Warfare took place in heaven on her behalf as I worshipped the King of Glory and prayed for her. You see, Madison's responsibility as a fourteen-year-old child was to follow the instructions of her parents. My responsibility as a mother, who believed in and knew the power of God, was to engage in spiritual warfare against principalities she was not yet equipped to fight. Consequently, Madison gained the victory over the many challenges she faced her freshman year of high school. So, when she asked me a couple of years ago if I worried about Joshua and Caleb's future, I laughed, and my response was "*No.*" My laugh was full of praise to the Lord because I remembered how He heard and answered every prayer concerning her. The same way He took care of her, He will care for Joshua and Caleb.

My prayers for Madison have not stopped and never will. The same prayers I've prayed for her, I pray for Joshua and Caleb. I know without a shadow of a doubt, the prayers of God's children have much force and yield good results; especially when those prayers are enveloped in the Holy Scriptures and promises of God. You may be facing a challenge that seems insurmountable and beyond your ability to resolve or overcome. We have all been there. Do you recall the conversation the Apostle Peter had with a group of wives when he encouraged them to posture their hearts with meekness and fearlessness? He said that this heart posture was of great value in the sight of God, and if they were to adopt this disposition then they would do well and would be considered the daughters of Sarah, the Mother of Faith.

You see, a woman who does well, or who is a well-doer, is not fearless because she possesses innate courage. No. She becomes fearless because she has learned to trust and connect with God the Father through prayer. Moreover, through the name of Jesus Christ, she has witnessed circumstances change and work for her greater good. She is a perpetual visitor to the throne room of God, always putting her prayer request before Him. She understands her consistent visits are not a nuisance to Him, for He delights in the prayers of the righteous.

> *The sacrifice of the wicked is an abomination to the Lord: but the prayer of the upright is his delight. Proverbs 15:8 KJV*

Most importantly, she believes in the divine law God has established that declares the active and present prayer of the righteous prevails and has much force. Frequent, determined, and fervent prayer always gets God's attention!

> *The effectual fervent prayer of a righteous man availed much. James 5:16 (b) KJV*

I liken the power and result of fervent prayer to a mother in the Bible named Rizpah. She was a concubine of King Saul and bore him two sons, Armoni and Mephibosheth. After King Saul's death, Armoni and Mephibosheth were executed in revenge for a misdeed their father, King Saul, committed against a people called the Gibeonites. The brothers were hung publicly on a hill during the barley harvest season and were left there to hang with no proper burial in sight. Their mother, Rizpah undoubtedly witnessed their death, and her heart, without question, was broken into a thousand pieces. The Bible says that Rizpah never left their side but spread sackcloth upon a rock and stayed on the hill with her boys throughout the entire harvest season. This season lasted ten months. For ten months, she watched the decomposition of her sons' bodies and stayed on the hill with them to ward off and prevent vultures from tearing at their bodies during the day and to keep ferocious animals from eating them at night. She knew her sons didn't deserve to be devoured, just like you and I believe our loved ones do not deserve to be devoured by life's circumstances.

Rizpah's tenacity, courage, and show of love became the talk of the town. While many admired her actions, undoubtedly there were others who criticized her. Fortunately, the news of her fervor and determination reached the ears of King David. He was so moved and impressed by her actions that he determined to give her sons a proper burial. Rizpah's unyielding determination got the attention of the king. Like

Rizpah, when you and I are determined, consistent, and unyielding in our prayers, we too get the attention of the King of Kings. Like King David, God moves on our behalf and fulfills our desires. Remember, the well-doer is fearless because of her unyielding faith and confidence in God found through prayer. Never stop praying!

PRAYER

Heavenly Father,

Thank You for the gift of prayer. The Bible says Your ears are open to the prayers of the righteous. Thank You for Jesus, who makes me righteous and grants me access to You, both day and night. Father, teach me to pray. Take me from glory to glory by means of prayer. Allow my heart to love prayer above all else, for it is in prayer that I find You. In Jesus' name I pray. Amen.

REFLECTION

1. For three days, set aside time during prayer to talk with the Lord concerning the subject of prayer.

2. Write down what He shares with you about prayer on the provided pages.

3. Implement the new strategies (because He will give you strategies if you ask) God gives while in prayer.

Day One

Regarding prayer, God shared with me the following:

_____

_____

_____

_____

_____

_____

_____

I will implement the following prayer strategy:

_____

_____

_____

_____

_____

_____

_____

Day Two

Regarding prayer, God shared with me the following:

_____

_____

_____

_____

_____

_____

I will implement the following prayer strategy:

_____

_____

_____

_____

_____

_____

Day Three

Regarding prayer, God shared with me the following:

_____

_____

_____

_____

_____

_____

I will implement the following prayer strategy:

_____

_____

_____

_____

_____

_____

Chapter Eight

The Well-Doer
PURSUES PURPOSE

I grew up on the Southside of Chicago. Now looking back, decades later, I appreciate its rich culture. I place high value on my sisters and brothers, better known as my neighbors, who helped shape my worldview. I reminisce, and I realize how I was surrounded by a community of people who were immensely talented, innovative, hardworking, and determined. The majority of my community were skilled at navigating rough waters and somehow winding up on top. From this beautiful culture God began to shape me for His plan and from this foundation launched me into His well-thought-out purpose.

We all are born both with and for a purpose. Purpose, being the reason behind your creation and existence. Purpose, being who you are and not necessarily what you do. What you do should simply be a byproduct of your essence. From the time of my birth, my grandfather would tell my grandmother that God had a special purpose for my life. He would often say, *"Loretta, she has a veil over her eyes,"* which was symbolic to him of the touch of God. Now, my grandfather was a wise Southern man, born and raised in the backwoods of Alabama. Back then, people in the South had deep and sometimes superstitious convictions by which they bullheadedly governed their lives. My grandfather's convictions often became law in our family.

Consequently, the sentiment regarding my purpose was often repeated by others in my family, which frequented my ears and eventually found a home in my heart. As a child, the thought of a higher purpose often felt restrictive, because it brought about a conviction that was present at every turn. Every decision was often accompanied by the voice of a family member expressing what good they expected of me, making my decisions weighty. *Will I choose good or bad? Who will I disappoint if I choose this path or that path?* While this birthed in me a false need to be perfect, which I later had to overcome, it also provided me with boundaries for which I am now incredibly thankful. Those expectations often kept me from making poor, life-altering decisions. Most importantly, the knowledge that I was born with purpose to fulfill was engrained in my heart.

No matter how the conviction of purpose was planted, the fact remains that I, like you, have a purpose and bear a responsibility to pursue it. I promise you, pursuit of your God-given purpose is well worth it, for in the end it will conclude with a "*Well done, good and faithful servant,*" from the Author and Creator of your life.

I have discovered that traveling well on this earth happens when you know who you are and why you are. When you finally come into true agreement with God regarding His purpose for you, you can then maneuver through life according to that knowledge and conviction. Although not always easy, you learn to make decisions and move absent of the opinions of others, simply because you know the reason for your existence, and if circumstances or certain paths do not support God's vision for your life, then you reject them. We sometimes neglect to realize how proud it makes the Father when we embrace the vision He has for our lives, and pursue it with our whole hearts. If you are a parent, you are familiar with what happens in the heart when your children follows the path and principles you have set out for them. Your heart beats **loud!** However, the volume of pride that exudes from you in this instance does not compare to the noise and celebration that takes place in God's heart when we take courage and pursue our purpose.

Do you recall the lives of Orpah, Ruth, and Naomi referenced in the Bible? Naomi was the widow of a Jewish man named Elimelech, who relocated his family from Bethlehem-Judah to the country of Moab due to a famine in the land. He and Naomi had two sons who married Orpah and Ruth, while sojourning in Moab. Unfortunately, in the process of time, Elimelech and his sons passed away, leaving behind Naomi and her two daughters-in-law. Heartbroken, Naomi eventually received news that the famine had ended, and the Lord had visited her homeland with sustenance; wherefore, she resolved in that moment to return home.

Before I go further, it is important that I interrupt this story and give you insight into the character of Naomi's daughters-in-law who decided to return with Naomi to her country. Orpah's name meant gazelle. Gazelles are known for their keen ability to hear, see, and smell, which is crucial to their survival. During Bible days, names were significant and often signified a person's place of origin, one's purpose, or character; therefore, with this truth, we can assume that Orpah, the gazelle, was a woman of discernment. Ruth's name simply meant friend. She was a faithful friend.

On their journey back to Bethlehem-Judah, Naomi turned to Orpah and Ruth and thanked them for the kindness they had shown her and her deceased sons. She went on to instruct them to return home to their families in hope that they would find soul rest and even perhaps a husband. The girls fiercely rejected Naomi's suggestions with tears, exclaiming they would not leave her.

Naomi continued on and built her case by saying, *"What can I give you? I'm old, unmarried, have no sons, and even if I were hopeful, married a husband today, became pregnant, and bore sons, will you realistically wait around until they became adults and marry them? No! Return home to your family and to your gods!"*

It was in this moment that Orpah, the woman of great discernment, listened to her core and intuitively determined that what Naomi said was true, her purpose was not with Naomi. Ruth, on the other hand, was a friend and understood that she was called to be a faithful friend to Naomi, even unto death. The Bible records that after Orpah's departure, Ruth clung to Naomi and was indignant in her determination not to leave her.

Ruth's response to Naomi's speech was, "Do *not tell me to leave you! Where you go, I will go. Your people will be my people and your God will be my God. May the Lord deal with me, ever so severely, if nothing but death separates me from you!"* You see, Ruth understood her purpose as a friend and relentlessly pursued it no matter the cost.

I love these two women, Orpah and Ruth, because they understood who they were, and absent the opinions of others, they pursued their individual purpose. Orpah and Ruth were well-doers who understood the reason for which they were created, and perhaps, even if they didn't understand in totality, they listened to the core of who they were. Orpah, a woman of keen discernment and Ruth, a faithful friend, were led by purpose. Will you do well, listen to your core, and pursue your God-created purpose, no matter the cost? A well-doer pursues her purpose.

PRAYER

Heavenly Father,

Before I was born, You knew me. While I was in my mother's womb, You fashioned me for Your delight and purpose. Thank You for Your great and intricate love for me. May Your purpose for me burn deeply in my heart. Give me the courage and strength to pursue purpose with all of my being. Make the path ever so clear. In Jesus' name I pray. Amen.

REFLECTION

1. What is your God-given purpose?

2. Are you walking in your purpose? If not, why? If yes, how?

3. Revisit God in prayer regarding your purpose. In this season, what are His thoughts concerning you and your purpose?

Chapter Nine

The Well-Doer
LOVES PEOPLE

There is an endless, melodious message that has resounded from heaven to earth since the beginning of time. A harmony that carries the sentiment that mankind is deeply loved by their Creator. We were created out of sheer delight, for the Bible says when God saw everything He had made, it was immensely good.

> *And God saw everything that he had made, and, behold, it was very good. And the evening and the morning were the sixth day. Genesis 1:31 KJV*

History tells the story of how mankind, Adam and Eve to be exact, violated God's law and consequently were ejected from the Garden of Eden, never to return. Sadly, the Garden of Eden is the place where they dwelt together with God, so eviction meant eternal separation from Him, not just for them, but for the entire human race. However, God, in His relentless love for us, devised a plan of salvation that would reunite us with Him while on earth and for eternity. The Bible exclaims that God loved the people of this world so much that He gave His only Son, so that everyone who has faith in Him will have eternal life. (John 3:16 CEV) This plan was always in God's heart. The Apostle Paul told the Christians in Ephesus that God had decided in advance to adopt us into His own family by bringing us to Himself through Jesus Christ, and this gave Him great pleasure. The perpetual theme in the events of creation, the fall, and rise of mankind, is God's uncompromising and adamant love for mankind. How precious is His love toward us, both individually and collectively!

It is interesting that God so loves the world, but it is often difficult for humans to like one another, let alone love. Now, I don't make this statement lightly and as a blanket statement concerning the love we have for one another. Our world has benefited immensely, simply because of the love we have shown one another. However, the fact remains that loving our neighbor is not always easy. Yet, it is God's second and most important commandment given to us; we are to love our neighbors as we love ourselves.

Jeremy and I married very young, he was twenty years old and I was nineteen. We were deeply in love and committed to one another. I would like to believe that our "honeymoon stage" lasted a very long time and beyond the average. We were surrounded by mature couples who selflessly encouraged us in our marriage and would share wise counsel for a successful marriage. Jeremy and I were determined to apply the wisdom we received both from people and from God through His Holy Scriptures.

I remember when the honeymoon stage began to wear off and we encountered our first impasse, which led us to seek counsel from our pastors, who were a husband and wife co-pastor team. We met with them together as a couple, but also had individual sessions with them. During one of my sessions with Pastor Teresa, I shared with her that Jeremy would sometimes retreat with silence after a quarrel, while I on the other hand wanted to "talk it out." This would drive me nuts and seemed to crush my heart into a thousand pieces.

Pastor Teresa patiently listened to my complaint and after I was finished, she kindly said, "*Sweetie, you need to ask the Lord to fortify your heart and make it strong,*" in order for Jeremy's silence not to have such a debilitating impact on my heart. This word of advice was a defining moment for me, because it provoked and taught me to care for my heart, while navigating a difficult season.

We discussed the same scenario during a counseling session that included both pastors, and Jeremy and I. Pastor Shaun admonished me concerning Jeremy's silence and its effects on me by saying, "*Honey, you have to allow Jeremy to go into his cave and come out when he's ready.*" He went on to describe the makeup of a man and how retreating was often necessary for him, to recalibrate and deal with the matter at hand. Mind you, they were not letting Jeremy off the hook, but the wisdom they shared with me was crucial. It taught me the principle of considering the posture of my heart, while understanding the heart and thought pattern of my husband. This principle arrested my selfishness. When Jeremy would retreat with silence, I would relentlessly try to get him to talk, which translated in his ears as nagging. The Bible says, "A nagging spouse is like the drip, drip, drip of a leaky faucet; you can't turn it off, and you can't get away from it." Proverbs 27:15 MSG.

So, as Pastor Shaun described, Jeremy retreated to a cave. I took heed to the counsel I received and allowed him to withdraw and what do you know...Pastor Shaun was right. In the times when Jeremy would retreat, I allowed him to go into his cave and like clockwork, he would come out a short while later and be ready to discuss the matter at hand. The sign of him vacating the cave was always preceded by the sound of him whistling. When I heard him whistling with cheerfulness, I knew his heart had recuperated and he was ready to talk. On the flip side, Pastor Shaun admonished him not to remain in a withdrawn state for a prolonged period of time, because it was not healthy for the marriage, nor was it healthy for the heart of his wife. Jeremy heeded his advice.

I share this story with you because Jeremy and I learned two things. One, consider the posture of your own heart. Whether you are right or wrong in a situation, there is always something you can do to improve your heart's posture. Two, do not be selfish: empathize, and be humble enough to consider the thought pattern, natural bend, and heart of the other person outside of your personal feelings and/or needs. Most of all, we learned a great lesson from God about loving our neighbor.

Jeremy's and my love continues to increase over the years because we have endeavored to understand one another objectively and from the lens of God. No, this is not always easy, but it yields a great reward and that is love. I have learned throughout the duration of our marriage that I am highly valued and loved by God, but so is Jeremy. God loves and values him equally as He does me. This truth provokes me to love Jeremy more and care for him properly, simply because he is highly valued of God. Having been a life coach and leader within many church organizations, I have counseled women who believed they had special favor with the Lord, which somehow gave them a pass to mistreat or neglect their spouses. They failed to realize that God loves their husbands equally and will always stand on the side of righteousness, even if it does not look like what we believe it should.

Case in point: when Jeremy and I married, I was a virgin and he was not. I was a novice concerning all things sexual, while he was not. Most notably, his sexual drive was through the roof! Or, at least in my mind it was. Early in our marriage,

95

this became a point of contention for us. Again, we found ourselves in the office of Pastors Shaun and Teresa for counseling. The greatest lesson I have learned thus far in my marriage was attained in that counseling session. The pastors began to talk to us about the internal workings of a male's sexual drive and the science behind it. They even gave us a book to read on the sexual anatomy of a man and woman. Therein, I discovered my husband's sexual appetite did not derive from greed and that sexual intimacy for him was crucial to his productivity, esteem, and much more. This knowledge shifted the paradigm of how I viewed sexual intimacy, frequency, and the benefits it yields to both partners. By the same token, Pastor Shaun encouraged Jeremy to exercise self-control and sexual discipline, because his sexual drive clearly outpaced mine. Heeding this advice was an expression of Jeremy's love toward me and an act selflessness. Understanding the science and emotion behind his sexual drive provoked me to extend grace and love him all the more. The importance of intimacy took on a new meaning for me, which brought harmony to our marriage.

These life stories and lessons bear witness to the fact that we are able to love our neighbors as God commands when we're willing to exercise humility and objectively understand our fellow man. Love is not selfish. Furthermore, God deeply loves your neighbor as He does you, and as a well-doer, your endeavor should be to love what and who God loves.

I am reminded of Esther, a Jewish girl who was the cousin and adopted child of Mordecai. Mordecai's Jewish ancestors had been taken from Jerusalem with the exiles to Babylon. Consequently, this was how Mordecai and Esther found themselves living in Persia, in the town of Shushan. During this time, King Ahasuerus was the ruling king of Persia. The third year of his reign, he gave a banquet for all his officials and ministers, to include military and government officials. This banquet lasted six months. At the close of the banquet, he decided to throw a weeklong party for everyone living in Susa. During the party, his wife, Queen Vashti, refused to obey an order from him, which caused him great embarrassment and resulted in her being dethroned as queen. Thus, King Ahasuerus sought a new wife throughout the province, and Esther was chosen for her striking beauty. I imagine this was a fairytale, dream-come-true experience for Esther. She never imagined that she, once orphaned, would become Queen of the empire where she and her ancestors were exiles. A true beauty from ashes illustration.

In the meanwhile, during Esther's fairytale life as queen, an unjust decree was initiated by Haman, the king's highest-ranking official, to destroy every Jew in the province. King Ahasuerus signed off on the decree because he was given unethical information by Haman, whom he trusted. With the king's stamp of approval, the Jews' fate was sealed. In desperation, Mordecai, solicited the help of Queen Esther, for she was the Jews' only hope of deliverance and exoneration. Mordecai implored Esther to speak with the king to expose Haman's wicked scheme. Esther was hesitant because the law of the land required the king to first summon someone to his presence, and to appear before him without permission could result in death, even for the queen.

Mordecai quickly responded to Esther's reluctance with perspective outside and bigger than her own: *"Perhaps God elevated you to the position of queen for such a time as this—to deliver your people."* With this new perspective, selflessness was evoked in her heart and a sacrificial love for her people was birthed. Esther's response to Mordecai was, *"I will go to the king, even though it's forbidden. If I die, I die."* Much to Esther's satisfaction, the king received her with great delight, and she was able to expose Haman's wicked plan, which ultimately exonerated and saved her people.

Thanks to Esther listening to the counsel of Mordecai, and even at the risk of her own life, she was able to see the value of her people all the more clearly. She valued them more deeply. Esther was a well-doer. Her bravery, selflessness, and most importantly, her love for her neighbor, will forever be etched in eternity. Herein is an example of the beauty manifested when we love our neighbors as we love ourselves. This type of love is sure to evoke a *"well done"* on that great day you and I will stand before our Maker.

> *...the second is like it: 'You shall love your neighbor as yourself.' Matthew 22:39 NKJV*

PRAYER

Dear Heavenly Father,

Oh, what great love You have for me and what great love You have for my neighbors! Help me to value and love my neighbor as I do myself. This is the second greatest commandment. Thank You for the family, friends, and strangers You have given me the privilege to love. In Jesus' name. Amen.

REFLECTION

1. Do you struggle to see your neighbors as God sees them? Why or why not?

2. In what ways can you better love your family?

3. In what ways can you better love your neighbor(s)?

Chapter Ten

The Well-Doer

LOVES GOD WITH HER WHOLE HEART

Loving God is an intentional act inspired by the Holy Spirit. If we were to ponder the course of our lives, we would locate countless occasions where God has attempted to awaken the God-consciousness that lives within each of us. He visits us and like a young lad, love-stricken and in hot pursuit of his darling, God woos us towards His love. The same sentiments God expressed to the Prophet Jeremiah concerning the Children of Israel when He said, *"I have loved you, O my people, with an everlasting love; with loving-kindness I have drawn you to me" (Jer. 31:3 TLB),* also applies to you and me. His love for us stretches long and is filled with kindness. Yet, like the

102

pursued darling of the young lad described above, the choice to respond to God's wooing is ours. The choice to love Him back is of our choosing.

Early on, I shared with you how I dedicated my life to Christ at the age of fifteen. This was a drastic turnaround for me and everyone noticed, especially my family. My behavior was perceived as abrupt and strange, because I lived a very disciplined Christian life. My mother was worried because I talked mostly of God and found more joy at the local church than engaging in typical teenage activities. She and others thought I was too young to be so serious. Now looking back, I was a bit serious and extremely contemplative. Yet, the reason behind my behavior was the simple fact that I had a sincere encounter with the Lord and had fallen deeply in love with Him. His tangible love wooed me, and I followed Him hard with each passing day. As I made the decision to pursue Him, He revealed more of Himself, which caused me to love Him with my whole heart.

Loving God with your whole heart simply means to love Him with all of the ability that you personally possess. At the age of fifteen, I loved Him according to the capacity of my fifteen-year-old heart. God said, "When you seek Me, you will find Me, when you search for Me with all your heart (Jer. 29:13)." I made a personal decision to seek Him; therefore, I found Him. In finding Him, I discovered many more treasures about Him, evoking a greater love for Him.

You see, loving God is a personal choice and an intentional decision. When you choose to love Him, it yields a reward that places you on a journey that you never want to discontinue. As you search, He reveals, and your love for Him begins to fill every aspect of your heart. One of the treasures you receive when you pursue God, is the ability to love Him. It is as if you are running, trying to catch Him, and once you arrive, He gives you a box filled with love. The love is enough to satisfy your own heart and enough to place back into His heart, as a gift from you to Him. Essentially, the ability to love Him comes from Him. The more you seek Him, the more you will find Him and love Him. The Bible confirms, we love Him because He first loved us (1 Jn. 4:19). On your life journey and as a well-doer, a person who endeavors to live life well, you should resolve to seek after the Lord that you may love Him with your whole heart.

I am reminded of Mary Magdalene, to whom Jesus showed great kindness. Mary was a woman who had a very troubled life. The Bible does not provide details regarding her upbringing, but it does state that she was possessed with evil spirits. People are not born possessed by evil spirits, but often fall victim to treacherous circumstances that lead to their captivity. I imagine her possession manifested as mental illness, and many other things too. To make matters worse, the Bible records she was also physically ill. Yet Jesus in all His busyness of ministry found her. Not only did He find her, but He delivered her from demon possession and healed her body. He loved her. Mary was so enthralled by His love that she became a dedicated follower.

As a matter of fact, when Jesus was crucified on the cross and His body was prepared and taken to a tomb by a man name Joseph, Mary Magdalene and another woman named Mary secretly waited at the tomb. Mary had come to deeply love Jesus and her love provoked her to pursue Him even after His death. When Jesus appeared to His disciples after death, Mary was the first person He revealed Himself to, and He charged her with the privilege of telling the other disciples that He indeed had risen, just as He said He would.

Mary's encounter with Jesus is an example of what happens when we respond to His wooing; He gives us treasures of love that we in turn, give back to Him.

Will you be a well-doer who pursues God and loves Him with all your heart? This is the greatest commandment of all, and it is the most rewarding. When we love Him with all our capacity, He will withhold no good thing from us; the greatest of which is Him. The well-doer loves God!

> *Jesus said to him, "'You shall love the Lord your God with all your heart, with all your soul, and with all your mind.' This is the first and great commandment. Matthew 22:37-38 NKJV*

PRAYER

Heavenly Father,

I love You. You deserve all of my love. Thank You for loving me first and teaching me what true love is. As I pursue You, may my love increase toward You with each passing day. In Jesus' name I pray. Amen.

REFLECTION

1. Why do you love God?

2. In what way(s) do you express your love to God?

3. Is there room for growth, as it relates to you loving God
    with all your heart? If yes, in what ways can you grow?

A Note To The Reader

As we come to the close of our journey together, I pray that you were inspired along the way to live your life well. Remember, a well-doer's life is not absent of challenges; but rather, she is intentional and determined to navigate her life according to God's precepts. A well-doer values the next life over the present; therefore, her steps are fixed toward the path that leads her toward her heavenly home. Above all, she eagerly awaits the moment when God the Father says, "Well Done!"

> *His lord said unto him, Well done, good and faithful servant; thou hast been faithful over a few things, I will make thee ruler over many things: enter thou into the joy of thy lord. Matthew 25:23 KJV*

Please Note: through principles abstracted from Scripture, the art of biblical story telling, and the use of personal life experiences, I aspired to convey the message of *Well Done*! When communicating biblical stories, I strived to make the characters come alive and cause their lives to materialize in your imagination. We peeped into the intimate moments of their experiences. Through prayer and extensive study, I endeavored to uphold the integrity of the biblical text, while using creativity to fill in the blanks. Thank you for joining me on this colorful journey.

—Tikita

Works Cited

(2020, 09 09). Retrieved from Macrotrends: https://www.macrotrends.net/countries/WLD/world/life-expectancy

American Heritage Dictionary of the English Language, F. E. (2016). *American Heritage Dictionary of the English Language, Fifth Edition*. Boston: Hougton Mifflin Harcourt Publishing Company.

Eidenmuller, J. M. (2001-Present). *American Rhetoric, Top 100 Speeches*. Retrieved from American Rhetoric: https://www.americanrhetoric.com/speeches/mlkivebeentothe-mountaintop.htm

Max Roser, E. O.-O. (2013). *Life Expectancy*. Retrieved from Our World In Data: https://ourworldindata.org/life-expectancy

CPSIA information can be obtained
at www.ICGtesting.com
Printed in the USA
LVHW031549100121
675965LV00004B/286

9 781632 217646